RIVER ROAD

RIVER ROAD

. . .

Wayne Caldwell

BLAIR

Cover design by Laura Williams
Interior design by April Leidig

Frontis: Brice Cooper, unsplash.com

Blair is an imprint of Carolina Wren Press.

The mission of Blair/Carolina Wren Press is to seek out, nurture, and promote literary work by new and underrepresented writers.

We gratefully acknowledge the ongoing support of general operations by the Durham Arts Council's United Arts Fund and the North Carolina Arts Council.

Library of Congress Cataloging-in-Publication Data
Names: Caldwell, Wayne, 1948– author.
Title: River road / Wayne Caldwell.
Description: [Durham] : Blair, 2024.
Identifiers: LCCN 2024010458 (print) | LCCN 2024010459 (ebook) | ISBN 9781958888353 (paperback) | ISBN 9781958888407 (ebook)
Subjects: LCSH: Blue Ridge Mountains—Poetry. | North Carolina—Poetry. | Mountain life—North Carolina—Poetry. | LCGFT: Poetry.
Classification: LCC PS3603.A438 R58 2024 (print) | LCC PS3603.A438 (ebook) | DDC 811/.6--dc23/eng/20240315
LC record available at https://lccn.loc.gov/2024010458
LC ebook record available at https://lccn.loc.gov/2024010459

For Anna and Wesley

CONTENTS

RIVER ROAD

Be Careful

You be careful, now. The last thing Posey said to me.
Not funny, like one day on my way to church
He said, *Be careful. There's Christians there.* (But maybe
That wasn't joking.) The afternoon before he died
He brought a bag of cherry tomatoes,
Little bursts of August sunshine in your mouth.
Them little tommy-toes has overrun my garden.
Tired of stepping on them. Enjoy.
He looked fine. A little tired, but fit.
Well, Miss Susan, I'll be getting on home. You be careful, now.
He tipped his cap and headed down the hill.
Next morning no woodsmoke, but it was high summer,
So I hoped he ate a cold breakfast
And I'd see him later. I didn't. He didn't
Answer his phone. I found him still in bed, still as death,
Still, still. That's been two years and I still miss him
Like an amputee misses her missing limb.
It's why I ditched Pole Creek for River Road. Nothing here
To remind me of Posey except the disease of memory
That sometimes grabs me with its frigid hands.
So I'm careful. Mostly. After all, a poet
Might lose her edge if she's too cautious.

Living Water

I loved my tight little house but after
He died I knew I could stay no longer.
Too many memories, associations—
Besides, Pole Creek had always been too far away to hear
     And I'd decided I really wanted to be near
Living water. Sounds to soothe me to sleep
At night. Not a fountain or what they call a "water event"
But a real creek or river, flowing naturally beside
Wherever I might decide to light.

Took a while. Nearly a year looking all over
Buncombe and Haywood and Madison. Everything
Seemed too dear, too close to neighbors,
Too steep to be anything but a goat farm.
     At last we found a place with hidden charm,
Remote, run-down (affordable!), on River Road
In Madison. Surrounded by Forest Service, one
Absentee neighbor, and the French Broad River. Perfect.

My realtor almost didn't show it for fear
I'd be put off by the loneliness and disuse.
Vacant over a year, it *was* rather daunting,
A potential money pit. But before I went inside
     I sat a while on the narrow porch to hear
The river's music and knew I needed to be here.
I could buy it with the money from my little house
And have plenty left over to make repairs, put in a new bathroom,
Dig a new well, and otherwise plant myself beside living waters.

After an offer I about broke my arm signing documents
Before they changed their minds. She sold my house
Quickly to a couple from Durham who feared
Their home might be seaside property in a decade or two.
          I moved to Madison after the well and bathroom too
Were finished, in October. Leaves were falling, just like embers,
Reds and golds and yellows and browns in season,
And, sitting on that porch, windbreaker 'round my shoulders,
Afternoon sun shimmering on living water, I was at peace.

Eagle Bluff

I think a house should have a name
That relates its inner nature.
Cup of tea in hand, I sit
On my narrow porch to think.
River *What*? River Cabin?
River Retreat? River Refuge?
Nothing rings remotely true.
Then a good-sized raptor lights
In a tree across the road.
White head, yellow beak,
Lord, a male bald eagle!
He looks downriver, then at me,
And takes off like a holy spirit.
That stops all my naming stuff.
Henceforth my house is Eagle Bluff.

This House

I've felt no ghostly presence here,
But have wondered many times
What went on in all these rooms.
The smiles, the tears, the loves, the hates
That families always seem to create.
Who was born here? Who died and why?
Did deacon ever darken that doorsill?
Anybody ever cheat? Steal? Lie? Kill?
Did they pray over dinner? Or hug each other?
Were there little girls who feared their mother?
Or angry boys afraid to smack their father?
Or simply dreamed over the Sears catalog
And wished for things to be much better?
Sometimes I wish these boards would mail me a letter.

Sunday Morning

On the porch, coffee, river singing incessant song,
I watch three black crows pick at some
Thrown-out thing, French fry, maybe cigarette.
(Do crows smoke? No, but I bet they chew.)
One hops backward as a fourth flies in.
Their gossip comes to me in scraps.
As a blue kingfisher rattles downstream
A silent silver heron lofts to dodge the din.
Several shrill blue jays mob a robber,
Wily blacksnake sneaking close upon their nests.
Finches chitter across the road like schoolkids.
All this bird talk softened by water on rocks,
Quick water, as these mountains call it,
A sound that, thank God, never takes a rest.

Old Gabe

At the old hardware in the rock building by Spring Creek
I said, *I need a handyman.* The clerk asked *Where at?*
The old Shelton place on River Road. He laughed.
You'll need more than a handyman. He looked me over.
Old Gabe's your guy if you can get him. He's right fussy
About who he works for. I nodded. *Do you have his number?*
Lady, he ain't got a phone. I sighed. *Where can I find him?*
He's been working a right smart up at the Jesuit House.
I thanked him and headed up the hill. Found an overalled man,
With curly hair and beard that in his youth had been red as fire,
Planing a rough board lying across two sawhorses.
He stopped, looked up at me, and smiled, blue eyes friendly, calm.
Can I help you? he asked in a kind but husky voice.
Are you the one they call Old Gabe?
He laughed. *Some call me that. Ain't from around here, are ye?*
My turn to smile. *I'm from near Winston-Salem. And you're not a bit old.*
I'm old in dog years, he announced, and chuckled.
What can I do for ye? That was a Thursday morning.
Monday he met me at home, reworked my doorjamb,
And hung two doors like he did such things in his sleep.
He's been working off and on here ever since.
I don't know his surname—I pay him with cash.
Don't know exactly where he lives. But sometimes
He brings me a jar of chowchow or pickled squash he's canned,
Or sourwood honey from his bees. Smarter than a crow,
He can figure anything out. And he's a man of even disposition.
I don't believe in predestination or God's Plan
For Everything, but if there were, to meet Old Gabe
Would be a great part of it. He's the reason this old house
Has become safe and snug. I'll happily finish my days here.

Walker

Walker Shelton rolled Prince Albert smokes
That he stuck in the corner of his mouth, lit,
And spit out when a threat to burn his lips.
Some folks never saw him without one,
Except in church, when his wife Ethel made him go.
He kept two sets of dogs, both mean as tarnation,
One at the house, the other on Huff Island, where he
Stilled his corn. Dogs didn't care for any human
Except Walker and Ethel, so when you stopped by
You didn't get out of the car. Walker appeared
At the fence like a smoke-faced spirit, asked if you wanted
Pint or quart or what. He'd come back directly
And trade it for cash money. Everyone was happy
And nobody got their legs chewed off.
It's his house I bought—and legacy, too.

Basement

Basement? Well, certainly not the full kind.
There is a small one on the west side, a can house mostly.
But the one in which the lizards live is underneath the porch.
A simple dug-out space with a front door, maybe
Sixteen by six in a stretch, and barely enough room
In which to stand. (Walker, I'm told, was short.)
In it he kept corn, sugar, needful things, you know.

One morning before dawn a revenue man, pistol out,
Snuck up to the house, getting by the dogs somehow,
Whether by a spell or a large piece of red meat.
He was nearly to the porch when a canine lunged
For his lightly trousered left leg—and missed.
The click of teeth in empty air inspired the man
To drop the gun and dive into the storage space.

When the dogs began raising hell, Walker came,
Saw the commotion, and conquered all merciful thoughts.
Grabbed his new pistol, locked the basement,
T-man, spiders, mice, and all. No food, drink, or privy.
Some twenty-four hours, fiercely guarded by embarrassed dogs.
Along about dawn, Walker and his twelve-gauge
Opened the door. *You so-and-so*, he said,
I orta kill you. Or let them dogs do it, one.
Walker pointed the shotgun at the whimpering man.
*If I put them dogs up, will you vow never to darken
My land again?* When Walker opened the door again,
I changed my mind, he said, *you need killing.*
He stepped inside and shot the ground a foot
Away from the man's considerably shaking boots.

Walker stepped out to watch. Took about a half hour
For the deafened man to poke his head out, smelling of bladder
And bowels and looking ready for Dorothea Dix.
Git, said Walker, and stood aside.

The Fed got. Ran across the road, tumbled over the bank.
Nearly fell in the river and drowned. Clambered back up
Through poison oak and headed lickety-split for Tennessee.
A half hour later, having remembered he left his auto
At Murray Branch, he sped back east. Walker grinned.
They said the man gibbered the best part of a day in his car.
Walker sold liquor that morning like nothing ever happened.

They tell that for the truth. I accept it as legacy.
From Walker Shelton to Susan McFalls. Priceless.

Central Heat

That first time Old Gabe came, he looked around,
Worked on the back doors, took a break midmorning.
He packed his lip with Skoal, looked at me,
Asked: *Ye fixing to overwinter here?*
I nodded. Fall of the year, nights already
Turning to what Daddy called "scrooching weather."
Miz McFalls, you'd be right sorry about that,
Way your place is.
Please, I said, *call me Susan.*
I might, oncet I get to know you better.
So you think to winter here's a lame idea?
He spat brown halfway to the road.
Don't know if ye looked in the basement,
But they ain't no furnace there no more.
I misdoubt that yard tank'd hold oil anyhow.
I'd bet they ain't a lick of insulation here.
And I'd say they ain't no flue in the chimbley.
You'd burn the place down using the fireplace.
Ain't no gas line out this way. Miz McFalls,
You got to find another place to lay your head
Or get you a heat pump, one. Seal off that fireplace.
Insulate the floors and walls and attic. That ain't the best—
You sure can't get warm with central heat—
But at least you won't freeze your toenails off.
My turn to nod. *Can you do all that?*
He smiled and spat. *Lady, I can do most anything.*

I never regretted spending that money.
But after that first winter, he rebuilt the chimney
And installed an airtight woodstove.
Old Gabe (and Posey too) was right about central heat.
I've been comfortable ever since.

Writing Studio (I)

Eagle Bluff—a perpetual work in progress.
The house was built by fits and starts,
So no two rooms agreed on floor levels.
A narrow kitchen crept along the back of the house
Like an unwelcome uncle. To its west lurked a bedroom—
East a dining room doubled as my study,
Tripled as rear entrance. Its door and screen
Were not the same size but had been hung anyway.
I write at night, so spaces atop and under shut doors
Attracted all manner of creeping and flying creatures.
(Main door open, screen door shut, even worse.)
For a short time I fended off wasps, moths, and flies,
Ladybugs. Click beetles. A hornet or two.
The biggest green katydid of the entire fall.
After a dragonfly chomped my finger as I flung it outside,
I snagged Old Gabe to rid me of this problem.
I figured the kitchen should come first but asked myself,
What's more important, words or food? Easy.

Bookcase

The old maple bookcase in the living room
Sits on the west wall beside my easy chair.
I'm not a book hoarder—libraries do that for me—
But I do keep old friends. Two Bibles,
King James and Revised Standard,
To keep check on one another,
And a concordance for searching therein.
A *Webster's* Tenth. A thesaurus. A *Chicago Manual*
Twelfth edition (they don't change much).
A *World Almanac*, 1995 (they don't either).
And, of course, a Strunk and White to keep me straight.
Several nature guides, to wildflowers and snakes
And birds and such. Anthologies of poems,
Both English and American. A complete Shakespeare.
Paradise Lost. Pilgrim's Progress. And the best
River tale, *The Adventures of Huckleberry Finn.*
Flannery's stories. Randall's poems. Wilma's
French Broad. And a select few books
I reread from time to time—*Look Homeward,*
Charlotte's Web, To Kill a Mockingbird.
My latest acquisition, perhaps my last,
Is Jane Kenyon's *Collected Poems*, a treasure.
If I wear it out, I'll have to get another.
Oh, on the top shelf a framed snapshot of Posey
Sits beside a green glass owl-shaped mug,
Full of pens and pencils, what he called writing sticks.
You never know when a poem might jump up to say hello.

Lizards

Lizards, I learned, aren't terribly friendly.
There were two, at least, that sunned
On the poured concrete steps up to the side of the porch.
The larger was a fence lizard, kind of an ordinary
Brown- and black-striped guy, bolder than his friend.
It would at least look at me sideways (do lizards look
Any other way?) a little while if I surprised it on the steps
Before it skittered up the side of the house or into
The dark basement. Its friend? I really don't know how close
Lizards become. A shy thing with a bright blue tail.
A skink, I learned, doesn't want to be looked at by humans,
Much less be picked up. They lose their tails rather than be captured.
(They grow back.) I never saw one in the house,
But was always amused to see them at the porch.
Good neighbors eat insects—and are very, very quiet.

Writing Studio (II)

New doors and windows meant I'd not
Be overflown by myriads. It's hard to write
With pen in one hand, flyswatter in the other.
This is only partly a pensive citadel,
But I *have* found brief solace here. Today
I wrote a small poem about a periwinkle,
The other day came one about a dandelion.
I'm working on a long poem about the river,
So to open the window to hear her
Is, as they say these days, "key." (A word
Strunk and White would disallow in that disguise,
But I doubt Huck would mind.)
This poetic nun frets not in her narrow room—
She doffs her shoes and hopes it's holy ground.

Fountain Pen

Folks ask do I write with a computer.
Never, I answer, as my inner eyes roll.
I scribble my drafts with a fountain pen.
The skritch of nib on paper tells me
I've gotten the rhythm right. Too, the smell
Of ink as it dries, and as it goes from bottle to pen
(I refill my cartridge with a syringe)
Plus inky fingers tell me I created well.
Call me old-fashioned, and maybe I am,
But no machine ever gave us green eggs and ham.

For Anita

Years ago a friend went to Calabash,
A town barely in North Carolina, famous
For fried seafood. It also boasts Callahan's, a gift shop
Which sells anything from hermit crabs to scrimshaw,
Golf shirts to swimsuits, postcards to corkscrews,
Where she bought me an orange-and-yellow plastic crab.
(Don't laugh.) It has ten legs—two in front, clawed—
Six stick out on the sides—then two behind.
It's some two inches high and four inches wide.
Each appendage is wired to the body by a spring.
He has lived on my writing table for decades.
(He?! Yes, of course, it's Claude Crab.)
When I type—or scribble—his little arms wiggle,
Great fun to see. So as I write, I smile,
And think of my friend, whose gift keeps me from being—
Well—
Crabby.
Some small things grow important as time goes on.

Periwinkle

Periwinkle boasts
Purple penta-petaled blooms
In my yard's corner.

Dandelion

No weed, but golden
Wine-giving sudden flower—
Harbinger of spring.

Trumpet Vine

Cow-itch to locals—
Beloved of hummingbirds—
I call it graceful.

Blue-Eyed Grass

No grass, but iris—
So small it hides yellow-eyed
Flowers in plain sight.

River Road

I don't own a TV set.
It's too much fun to porch-sit
And watch the traffic up and down
River Road (and down the river,
Itself a road, but that's another story).
This byway goes northeast five miles to town,
Southwest one mile to Tennessee.
Jeeps, pickups, sedans, mud buggies,
Slow, fast, loud, quiet, either bound
For something or coming back.
It was once a drover's road,
Full of hogs and turkeys in season,
Thousands of them by here every day.
I sit and think of sound and smell,
And wonder how that ever worked.
How many head of driven stock
Have ever passed this point?
Most all these days will run on gas,
But around the Fourth a mule train comes up
From Tennessee to Carolina and back.
One year a mule died in her traces
Near the house. They had to send a truck
To take her home for equine burial.
Some say it's bad luck to site a home
Too close to roads like this. (Don't ask a mule.)
But I think it's quite the opposite.
This road and Susan get along just fine.

Snakes

River Road is hard on snakes. I guess
They cross the road for water in dry times.
I've seen flat copperheads, black snakes,
Corn snakes, garter snakes, king snakes.
So far, no rattlers. I wouldn't go so far
As to say folks deliberately run them over,
But I suspect that happens.

Tonight I saw my first flat green snake.
Made me think of my old friend Posey,
Who lamented not having seen one in forever.
Posey, they are still here, I'll have you know,
Except one fewer around here tonight.
Where there's one snake, there's at least
One more, in Nature's providential way.

Metes and Bounds

Eagle Bluff sits on the western end
Of a tract a bit more than four acres,
On the property's only level spot.
The river is the south boundary.
Just north of the road beside the river
Is electric company right of way,
So is useless except for snakes and towhees,
Plants and bees. That's fine with me.
The plat is oddly shaped, a trapezoid
Awkwardly bent at each angle.
The east and north borders are marked
By Forest Service signs, the first of which
Is over a Geodetic Survey medallion
And a notice it's a bear sanctuary border.
The rest are plain markers on boundary trees,
Which are second growth, because two logging roads,
Probably cut when lumber barons were raping
Our mountains (and we all helped), snake up the mountain
On the back of the property. The last marker
Is in line with the little branch on the west side
That flows into the river when weather is wet
And dries up in the long hot summer. I suppose
I could clear a logging road and notch
Out a house site on the side of the mountain,
But why? I'm happy here,
And so are the bears and the birds. Besides,
The land lays such that I'm not bothered
By pesky developers who offer peanuts
For land on which they want to build
Sixteen McMansions—and call it Olde River Pointe.

The Pistol

When I moved in, I attracted attention.
Some of it welcome, like the friendly man and his dog
Who jogged by a couple of mornings a week.
Others, not so much, in rust-bed pickup trucks
Slowing by, trying to peer up the bank
To get a load of me. They didn't resemble choir boys,
Especially Friday or Saturday just at dusk,
Pint or six-pack beside, rifle racked behind.
Daddy taught me target shooting years ago,
So I drove to Asheville to purchase a pistol.
Had to wait for the sheriff to issue a letter
Saying I was a person of "good character."
(This from a man later imprisoned
For various federal crimes.) I got a Ruger nine-millimeter,
Fifteen-shot magazine, four-and-a-half-inch barrel.
I could actually hit something with it.
The slowing-down-at-dusk routine stopped
After I used that time to plink targets out back.
That I blasted cans as well as made racket
Was a message even stupid men understood.
(I call her Annie, as in Annie Oakley.
She sleeps in the night table beside me.)

Geese

When the river's low, geese settle for an afternoon
Across from the house, honking and feeding
Among the rocks. The gaggle will gabble
About whatever weighs on goosely minds.
Which I guess would not be much more than food and . . .
There's a spot upriver of almost always calm water,
Where one can often spy a dozen or more,
Looking like they walk on the water.
Jesus geese, I call them.
There's nothing holy about goose poop,
But when I hear a Whitmanesque *ya-honk*
I'll soon see one or more flying geese
Doing exactly what God made them to do.

More Geese

Not long after I moved to Eagle Bluff
Old Gabe was weatherproofing windows.
We enjoyed a break on the porch
When a V of geese y-honked and headed upstream.
He nodded to where the birds had been.
Know why one side of the V is longer'n t'other?
The poet in me thrilled to hear mountain wisdom
Given as if inscribed on stone tables.
Expectant, excited, exultant, I said, *Why?*
More geese, he deadpanned, headed back to work,
As if I were too simple to figure that out.
I had to laugh—what he said was exactly right,
But this silly goose sure didn't see it coming.

French Broad River

(With Apologies to Wilma Dykeman)

1

I've heard it's one of the oldest rivers in the world.
How they know that is mystery, but it looks old,
As if it could have carried—and probably did—
Rafts of indigenous prehistoric people
Proudly searching for the next good thing.

In the time before names, the river harbored
Beavers and bears, catfish and coons, herons and deer,
Eagles and skunks, mayflies and bats, big black cats
And packs of wolves, some of which, much later,
Folks patiently tamed until they turned into dogs.

The ancient people called the river "the Long Man,"
Fed by his chattering children—Swannanoa, Cataloochee,
Nolichucky, Hominy, and Wayeh, to name but a few.
This wet, widening road would have taken the Cherokee
Clear to salt water, had they cared to go.

DeSoto crossed it in the sixteenth century, some thirty-three miles
Due west of here. But, finding no gold, he moved on.
The Cherokee used it for food and transportation
Until white "settlers" encroached, and the government
Treaty-tricked and force-marched most of them to Oklahoma.

I expect dark travelers sped along on it at night,
Heading to underground railroad stations across the Ohio.
And on their heels slave-catchers bound to bring them back.
Wartime saw soldiers both in blue and gray
Cross and recross, exploding and rebuilding bridges and trestles.

Bridges served feet, hooves, teams, carts, wagons.
But trestles came to mean support for trains.
Heavy machinery to carry people and goods
Far and wide in postwar North Carolina.
In 1882 one could go from Asheville to Newport by rail.

Progress.

The tracks attracted factories beside the river, making things
And spewing waste into its waters. Paper mills,
Textile plants, tanneries, abattoirs, fertilizer plants,
Battery makers. By the mid-twentieth century,
You name it, it flowed into the poor old dying river.

Not to mention that everybody seemed to be moving
To the mountains, into houses in towns and cities
That sent raw sewage straight into the river.
Water, no longer blue or green but brown and gray
And black and lumpy, smelled to high heaven.

It's better now. The sixties and seventies saw vast improvement
In environmental law. Forty or fifty years later, fish
Can now be eaten safely, eagles have returned,
And during dry weather I can see the bottom
All the way across to Huff Island. This is real progress.

Now the river's travelers are rafters, canoers, kayakers,
Boaters, fishers, nature lovers of all kinds.
And, of course, the occasional deer crossing
Or kingfisher catching fire or goose ducking for weeds.
From my porch I watch it—once again, it is good.

11

The French Broad, being a river, floods.
How many times over millennia has it left its banks
And moved whatever was swept up in it
To some faraway (and sometimes ridiculous) place?
Perhaps thousands. And each time it returned to its placid face.

The worst (in the last century) was in July 1916.
Asheville's Riverside Park was washed away,
Parts of which one could have seen rushing by my house
Had it been here then. (Even this relatively high ground
Would have been inundated for several days.)

Only a half dozen people died in Asheville,
Which I'd consider a small miracle. Thanks to the telephone,
Warning came to Marshall, and only two or three drowned,
Even though the courthouse was about the only thing left
On Main Street. Fifty-three houses disappeared.

From high ground one could have seen rushing by
Bales of cotton, houses, mules, gas tanks,
Vehicles, sheds, chickens roosting on pieces of roof,
Tires, fences, trees, pigs, dogs, cats,
Anything not tied down—and many things that were.

I was here in 2001, the year the bridge over Paint Creek
Washed into the river. The water didn't flood the house,
But it sure tried. I watched logs and unmanned boats
And doors and walls and, once, a whole section
Of metal lockers, I guessed, from a school.

The river is mostly calm, but memory of its rampages
Stays in one's mind. I keep a "flood kit" handy

In case I have to hightail it downstream.
It's only a matter of time before another big one,
From which there will be no endurance—or flood insurance.

Meantime the river breaches banks more often,
Forcing DOT to close the road where pavement ends.
Posey predicted more heat and storms, and he was right.
Staying here is not without its share of worries,
But I'm thankful to learn to live beside the Long Man.

The Bible teaches the rainbow promise—never again
A worldwide flood. It also tells us God forgets.
Which, when I think about it, is pretty scary.
But I can't see God forgetting her river,
The ancient, wild, temperamental French Broad River.

Huff Island

Huff Island, some few acres of territory lying
Like an anchored ship in the river opposite my house,
Has a history full of tales. I only know two.
They say old Walker Shelton made his liquor over there—
From water from a spring behind my house piped
Under road and river, straight to his still.
DOT happily kept this system up in return
For his wares. I'd like to have seen that.
They also say a Captain Huff, a century before,
Drilled and trained the Rebel troops
Of the North Carolina Sixtieth there.
Hence, I guess, the name.
I'd like to have seen that, too.
An island with a history of military maneuvers—
And whiskey. Which often go hand in hand.
Now it's forested, quiet, and creatured.
Early this morning I watched four deer
Come down to the river to drink.
That is an improvement, I think.

Paint Rock (I)

I climbed it twice, just after I moved here
And my knees mostly tolerated steep.
A tough climb, steeper than Pisgah top
But not nearly as long. Up top
Is a great place to rest and watch the river
Curve toward Del Rio like a sometimes muddy
Old man bent on some lonesome journey.

The second time was high summer, a muggy day
When I wanted to wring out my sweaty shirt.
But a sudden breeze cooled me, and before I could react
The sky darkened and thunder said, *I'm a mere mile away.*
For some fifteen minutes the storm drenched me.
Lightning and thunder shook the mountain
Like God running full tilt on her way
To overthrow the wicked sinners in Newport.
I felt lucky to have escaped with only a soaking,
And the remembrance of a still, small voice
Telling me my exact place in her creation.
I'll not be up there again except in memory.

Old Daffodils

Most of the land east and north of here
Is owned by the Forest Service. It used to be
Farmland—pasture, orchard, woodlot, a goodly land
That yielded its fruit in season. The bottomland
Near the river now grows hay, but that's all.
Bear and deer and turkeys enjoy a rich place
In which to live and forage.

Up the road from here is a farmhouse,
What's left of it, a couple of walls
With broken windows, a bare foundation,
Half a roof. I wonder who first lived there.
I imagine a farmer's wife, proud of her
New cinder-block home with (maybe)
Central heat (or at least a good oil stove).
I know she loved it because every spring
The now grown-up bank that was her front yard
Blooms with old-fashioned daffodils,
The ones I call scrambled eggs, bulbs
Planted with her worn, rough hands decades ago,
Smiling, wishing these flowers to outlive her
And cause passing strangers also to smile
And perhaps to wonder who she was—
A kind of memory, another way we last.

Brighten the Corner

Fish live in the prettiest places.
I live in one, too. I walk the river road
Every day the weather allows. I love to see the breeze
Feather the leaves—a wooly bear's comic hurry—
The buttery flutter of a goldfinch, but . . .
In and beside the roadside ditches . . .
Cigarette packs. Beer cans. Snuff tins.
Tin cans. Fast food debris. Plastic bags.
And some stuff I'll not name in a poem.
What's wrong? Are some humans so flawed—or careless—
Or mean—or stupid? I certainly don't know.
Ole Fred said brighten the corner where you are,
So when I walk I carry a trash bag, gloves,
And a blue-and-white reachy stick.
(My work is picking up. Hope the fish notice.)

Fishing

You'd think, living here, I'd learn to fish.
Oh, I know how. At least Daddy tried
To teach me, at a farm pond—cane pole,
Worm bucket, cork float, patience.
I never saw much sense in it. Certainly
It wasn't good for the fish, down there
Minding their own business like God made them
To do. And I never liked to eat them,
Not once a fish bone stuck in my throat.
There are men (and an occasional woman)
Who park somewhat east of here and throw out two
Or three or four lines, and sit in a folding chair
All day. I suppose they just need to get out
Of the house a while and are blessed
With peace and quiet and a catfish or two.
Me, I'll let whatever's in the river stay there
And thrive. I'll just read another book.
Take another walk. Enjoy the flowers.
And listen to the magic music of a river full of fish.

Frog Optimism

First of February, quiet afternoon, walking
West toward Polecat Branch. Rainy and mild
The last few days, water standing in ditches.
Suddenly I hear what I think are geese,
Clacking their beaks against some unseen enemy.
But it's not at the river, where the feathered ones
Raise their usual ruckus. As I get closer
The roadside racket suddenly stops
And I hear several splashes in the ditch.
Frogs! Beside where they skittered
Float clumps of just-laid eggs, not yet strung out.
(So they "lay" eggs, but I didn't know
They "cluck" when it happens. A noise made,
I can only think, by optimistic frogs.)

Note: Aristophanes said frogs chorused *brekekekex-koax-koax*. That's
close to what I heard, but his were mostly satiric. Or at least cynical.

Tadpoles

In River Road's ditches surprising strings
Of dark-laced eggs appear late February,
Early March, harbinger eggs, I call them.
Within two weeks, given sun and rain,
Hundreds of little commas swim
In the syntax of ditch water, tadpoles
(Not polliwogs as my girl books said)
They are called. How many will become frogs?
Not many. It's a fragile place.
But I still thrill to see life begin,
Even as I lace my parka against the wind.

Paint Rock (II)

The Painted Rock was sacred to the Cherokee—
At least that's one speculation
About the pictographs on its face.
Another theory holds that they are road signs
To the hallowed warm springs upstream.
Whichever, I know it's holy to me,
And has been for countless others.
These days it's something of a tourist thing, too.
(A hollow fake rock in the yard covers my well.
One day I was mowing when a car
Full of tourons stopped. Pointed
Cameras ready, they asked "Is that the Paint Rock?"
I mouthed "No" and wondered how in the fire
Such pitiful people had found their way that far.)

The painted rock has witnessed everything, I suppose.
Drovers, hikers, evildoers, lovers, poison oak getters.
Every now and then a young daredevil gears up
To climb the sheer rock face with ropes and such.
I shake my head and hope he has no spray paint
Like the idiots who cover the ground level
With initials and obscenities. They ought to be shot.
Or, better still, be made to clean the rocks.
With a toothbrush. Then be shot.

One could argue that's a bit too tough,
But sometimes I think it isn't tough enough.

Beavers

Before I moved to Eagle Bluff
I didn't know much about beavers, except
They ate tree bark, built dams
That turned creeks into ponds—
And were trapped almost to extinction
Because beaver hides made excellent hats—
Plus, on old TV they sold Ipana toothpaste.
(That was Bucky Beaver, best I remember.)
Of course, they were always busy, at whatever
Beavers do besides eat tree bark.

Here, I learned that they live in the river
And come out at night to cross the road
And prune young saplings to drag home
To Mother, or whomever needs them.
Some beavers are either ambitious or dumb.
A gum tree near the Old Daffodil House
Has been gnawed on for months. The trunk's
A foot thick, and he (I can't imagine it is a she)
Is about halfway through it. I vote for stupidity.
Makes me wonder what problem poor Noah had
With his two beavers. As children we learned
The Lord told Noah to build him an arky arky
And build it out of sticks and barky barky—
And back then there was no Purina Beaver Chow.
So he'd have to check for leaks every night.
Anyway, I'm glad they are in the river now,
And equally happy I don't have to eat tree bark.
But why do they harvest their food in the dark?
I guess they don't want anyone to see them,
In case some mean creature might try to tree them.

Wildlife

When walking River Road I see and hear
Rabbits, groundhogs, squirrels, and deer,
Eagles, kingfishers, herons, and crows,
And birds that warble and finch and tweet.
Tonight I hadn't gone far from the house
When I chanced to have a talk with a mouse.
Modest gray fur ball crouched in the road
Stared up with bugged-out black eyes.
You're going to make a snake a snack, I said.
It seemed confused. I tapped my foot—
The tiny rodent looked to run up my leg,
Then skittered behind a rock instead.
Have a nice evening, I politely said
And walked on down to Polecat Branch.
As I returned, the addled fool was back
In the road. *If you stay out too late,
You'll be snatched up by a silent owl.*
I swear it seemed to grasp the fact
It was a minor link in the world's food chain.
It scurried off to home. Only, I thought,
To be grabbed by some old famished fox.
(You know, I never did much care for mice.)

Ironweed

Queenly color dark
Fall's appointed herald sings
The end of summer.

Asters

Autumn's assurance
That winter won't do us in.
Bees are happy, too.

Chicory

A pure blue presence—
What we do all love to have—
Except in coffee.

Jewelweed

Don't touch the jewelweed
Unless you have poison oak
Or just love beauty.

For Randall Jarrell

I took Modern Poetry my second year
At Woman's College, as they called it then.
Enter a slender man with full black beard,
Sporting tweeds and, of all things, an ascot.
With sparse preface he began to read
To us in a singsong voice powered by
An enthusiastic love of language.
Scared me to death. *I have to remember*
All this? Wasn't long until we knew a lot
About Frost and football and Eliot and cats
And Moore and Rilke and Proust and Nash
And Prokofiev and Mahler and Whitman and Yeats.
And tons of arcane lore that overflowed
From the deepest mind I've ever known.
His class was like a fast ride in his black MG.
He's why I set out to be a poet.
When I heard he had died, I cried and cried
And asked that Death be kind to this man I loved.

Fog

This morning Eagle Bluff was wrapped in mist,
Quiet, thick as cat fur, twice as soft.
If this fog came in on little cat feet
They belonged to a huge old puss, for I
Could barely see the river, forget Huff Island.
Sandburg raised goats, but hooves make racket,
And we know his wife raised Siamese,
So the Chicago poet gave us feline feet,
Padding in a proper parade of poetic mousers.
Their mom (or dad) was Herriman's Krazy Kat,
Who begat Marquis's immortal Mehitabel,
Who danced paw in paw with Sandburg's foggy beast.
Then came Old Possum's mystery cat Macavity,
Followed by Jarrell's old Kitty (a Persian pet I really met),
Who was dogged by Chappell's familiar, Chloe.
A poetic praxis I'll likely not continue,
But if I should, she'll be called—who else, but Fog.

Fleas and Ticks

Marke but this flea—Jarrell began one day,
Donne, with this line, he came to say,
Slapped all prior love poems in the face. Then he
Jumped ahead to "Prufrock," whose *patient*
Etherised upon a table did the same for his time.
Jarrell smiled. Puffed up, he broke out in rhyme.
I'm working on a poem about a bat.
I wrote the rough draft while my cat
Sat in my lap, dreaming no doubt of eating a rat.

It had no norm-shattering lines (as no doubt
He hoped we'd hear). Its ending was soft clout.
All the bright day, as the mother sleeps,
She folds her wings about her sleeping child.
We girls oohed, which almost made him mad.
As today's poetry goes, it isn't half bad.
I made a note to write about a tick,
Which years later Posey thought a little sick—
I like it, though—it's a clever little trick.

God's Time

After my supper I like to walk,
Makes my belly much less likely to talk
When I'm falling asleep. So I don't much like
The switch in the fall when clocks will strike
An hour off from the day before,
So after the meal I can't go outdoors.

Posey didn't much care for DST
Either. Said he grew up most carefree
Without it. EST he used to call
"God's Time," though it isn't mentioned at all
In the Bible, unless the Jericho sun
Can be construed to forerun.

One or the other, I say to keep,
So we always know to fall asleep
At the same time of a night. Then Spring
Forward and Fall Back will not be a thing
We have to remember, leaving more room
In our brains for lovely ideas to bloom.

Solitude

I had three chairs in my house, one for solitude, two for friendship,
three for society. —Henry Thoreau

I had three porch chairs at Uncle Ike Hill:
One for me, one for Posey, and one we set aside
For Birdie, as the Seder keeps a place for Elijah.
Here at the river, two will do. Old Gabe and I
Use them to advantage, telling stories
And being quiet, watching the river's humors.
(Friendship means you talk—or not—
And all is well. I don't mind him
Spitting off the porch. I have to think it is
Somehow beneficial to certain plants.
Or deadly to certain insects.)
Don't get many other visitors. Jehovah's Witnesses
And Mormons don't come this far downstream.
Have not entertained a visitor wanting my vote.
Or a trick-or-treater. Every decade a census taker comes,
And for a while a guy brought the phone book
When they still printed them. A random visit from the church.
That's about it, which suits me perfectly. I don't care
For commotion. As long as I have the river,
My books and paper and ink, I'm not lonely.
(Which is a word for teenage love songs.)
Had no neighbors until someone subdivided
Land downstream, sold some lots, and made
A riverside commons for something called
A Homeowners Association. They invited me to join,
But why pay to be there in summer crowds,
With boom boxes, grills, coolers, and such?

I was polite. They probably think me aloof
Or arrogant, but I'll stay here like that old
Hypocrite Thoreau stayed in his little house
With three chairs. (He managed only two years
Before deciding town living had its benefits.)
I'm here for the long haul. And I love it.

Rafters

These days the folks who ride the river come
In a variety of vessels, and range in age and dress
And shape and size. Some are solitary,
In johnboats or kayaks, or homemade crafts
Requiring bail buckets as standard equipment.
There are groups, some tied together by guides
And inner tubes, kids from summer camps
Or families taking Mother for a river ride.
There are couples, men showing off for their mates,
Women keeping watch in the bow or in their own boats.
(Perhaps with their dog, or dogs.) One afternoon
A lone woman in an open boat towing a small raft
With a cooler inside floated by. She wore sunglasses. That was all.
People ask if I enjoy rafting. I say I'd rather watch.
I have plenty adventure on the porch, pen in hand.

Tongs of Fire

One hot summer our little Arcadia Baptist Church
Held a revival. I was five or six. The preacher
Was a runty red-haired man with fiery eyes
And Pentecost on his mind. One night he brought a pair
Of blacksmith's tongs. Steel. Wicked-looking pincers.
He was no preacher to stay aloof in the pulpit.
No, he roamed the aisles, tongs in hand,
Shouting about how hot—and long—and awful
Hell will be. *Imagine,* he said, *you get down there*
And the Devil gives you these to keep forever.
They heat up quick, but you don't get no gloves.
You got to pick up one by one a half-mile pile
Of fiery rocks and carry them across a wide, burning river.
You get through, then you got to tote them back again.
Over and over and over for all eternity. He stopped by our pew,
Raised himself to a full five foot four, and yelled
How do you avoid this awful judgment? REPENT!
And stuck those tongs up to my face.
I screamed bloody murder and didn't know
Which was worse, the thought of hell,
Or knowing he'd made me wet my drawers.

Although my mother said he meant well,
I know that if there is a hell
He's there, handling those tongs of fire.

Three Days in a Whale

Twelve or thirteen I was when I heard
A sermon depicting the Christ as God's word.
Saint John said without Him nothing was made,
Then He came to earth and all our sins paid,
Scourged, mocked, spat upon, nailed to a tree,
He hung there and died just for you and for me.

My poor youthful mind asked *How can this be?*

From that day my Bible I earnestly searched,
But what I found tore me away from the church.
Three days in a whale—the sun standing still—
God came to Egypt all firstborns to kill—
All those animals fit into one small boat—
And Elisha made a borrowed axe-head float.

All of these things in my mind I rewrote.

When Abraham became a century old,
Sarah gave birth to Isaac, we're told.
The boy to his father could do no wrong,
But one day the voice of the Lord came along—
Kill me a son, Abraham thought he had heard,
All of which seemed profoundly absurd.

(He was old! He likely heard the wrong word.)

This woman still cannot find any worth
In the strange old creed of sweet virgin birth.
But older, I now see plenty of truth
In such ancient yarns as the story of Ruth.

I'm at an age I can be more believing,
And hear a story without it unweaving.

Sometimes your mind interferes with receiving.

So there's calming the sea—turning water to wine—
On the mountaintop seeing His face to shine—
Time and again many people are healed—
But commanded sternly that He not be revealed.
Many a tale we are told about Jesus
I stretch to believe—but at least now it pleases.
(And note: I refuse to rhyme *Jesus* and *diseases*.)

Heaven

Don't know if there's a heaven, at least
Not what Posey knew, where he was sure
He'd be reunited with Birdie forever.
I don't have that vision (or clarity).
But I do know, or think I do, that something waits
Us after death. And I hope it is far, far better
Than anything mortals can imagine. Paul says
We will be changed, in the twinkling of an eye.
We'll become energy, light, whatever quarks are,
Part of the mind of God, whatever that means.
As Mother Julian said,
All shall be well,
And all shall be well,
And all manner of thing shall be well.

About the Best That I Can Do

I used to be an optimist. Began that way, cradled in the Jesus story. Parents said I could be anything I aspired to be. I wanted to study engineering at N.C. State. But I was female, so settled for an English major at Women's College. So there was that. I loved Sinatra and Dorsey. When the Beatles and Dylan appeared, I learned a new song, but then came rap and Metallica and such. So there was that. I liked the Trumans (especially Bess), was only mildly irritated at Ike and Mamie, and loved the Kennedys. But then came Oswald, Viet Nam, Nixon, Kent State, enough to shadow anyone's sunniness. It hasn't gotten any better, what with 9/11 and the "war against terrorism," "the war against drugs," torture in prisons, name it, we've stepped in it. I worry that soon we'll flirt with authoritarianism or worse. So there's that.

It looked in the forties and fifties like we were determined to kill off any number of animal species. Then came Rachel Carson. (A woman, remember.) Now brown pelicans fly over the beach and bald eagles soar at the river. (Even Nixon ["I'm not a Crook!"] signed the EPA into law.) So there's that. Now, there's global warming, climate change, whatever one calls it. I used to share the Enlightenment view that science and engineering will eventually fix anything. Not sure of that anymore. Look now at what all's endangered: tigers, elephants, giraffes, polar bears, lions, penguins. And what we have too much of: oriental bittersweet, multiflora, kudzu. Nutrias. Armadillos. So there's that.

Yet, there's Jesus. Whose story, however strange and hard to believe, is one of ultimate optimism. That's really the whole story line of the Bible. That Jesus was present at creation and will be present again at the end time. Even from the exile we feel we are in, when quotidian things seem insurmountable, we will learn somehow to sing a new song, and at the end, all will be well. I think I do believe that. I have to believe that. It's about the best that I can do right now. So there's always that.

Prayer

(With Apologies to George Herbert)

Prayer, an open book, a chord of grace—
The breath of God, a quantum leap—
A pound of nard—a holy place—
A coin found—recovered sheep.
A garden locked, a fountain sealed—
An eagle's skree, a solar wind—
Thanksgiving feast—Christ revealed—
Still, small voice—of a friend.
Joseph's mousetrap—noisy gong—
A parable grasped, the river's air—
Waters of life, God's good care—
The voice in the cloud—salvation's song.
A flame of fire—the soul's wood—
A poem written—what she could.

Crystal River

Today our guest preacher, a young man
Fresh from seminary, somewhat stringy-haired, but cute,
Took a text from John of Patmos, where a crystal river's tide
Forever flows by the throne of God. Yes, he gathered
Us at the River—that would be Jordan—with Jesus—
Then waded back to Psalm One, where a riverside tree
Yielded its fruit. Whew. I wanted to lay my every burden down
And walk the margin of my French Broad River.
But he quickly moved us to Exodus, where Moses
Whacked a rock, from which water flowed.
My wrinkled forehead said, that's a water fountain,
Not a river. But then he hauled us to Saint John,
Who (the boy claimed) said or at least implied the soldier
Piercing Jesus' side became Moses, and Jesus
Was the rock giving that grace-filled day both a river
Of living water (baptism) and blood (communion).With Huck, that
    was too many for me.
But somehow he managed, after a few more verses
I now forget, to fly us back to Patmos,
Where flashed a crystal clear message: all things
Will be made new, and death shall be no more.
I have to say, he landed that sermon smooth as seaplane on river,
Where bright angel feet have trod. I was impressed, if exhausted.
Well, he's young yet—he'll learn, the Gospel is simple—Grace
    abounds.

Church

Yes, I said "guest preacher." That implies
I have a regular pastor and am involved
In a church. That's mostly or at least partly right.
I attend the Methodist church in town
Every now and then—and even drop a little money
In the collection plate. But my true church
Is with the river and its choir—
Water over the rocks is organ music
And heron and eagle and deer and geese
Are preacher and acolytes and elders.
I've nothing against "organized religion"
And, like Posey, read my Bible almost every day.
But, with the psalmist, I rejoice in the day
The Lord has made, and am glad in it,
In my place beside the river of the water of life.

Goose Grass

Nature sometimes plays games with her creation,
Providing the unexpected—a white squirrel—
An egret instead of the usual heron—
A barred owl in broad daylight—quite a nice sensation.

But there's weeds, one of which makes me madder'n hops.
Goose grass. Catchweed. Bedstraw. Sticky Willie.
A plant with many forms, disguises, and names.
You think you've pulled it all—then out a new bunch pops.

I once asked Posey to name its mountain face.
He shook his head and smiled like I had asked
A rainbow trout to leap clean up into a clear blue sky.
He said, *I call it the ---- that takes the place.*

Lord! Just found another patch—I can't believe it!
I guess one day I'll simply have to die—and leave it.

Ladybugs

Don't much think that ladybugs think—
But in September they seem to think
They'll overwinter in my bedroom.
Sunny afternoons I'll see a few on the windowsill,
Then in a half hour a hundred or more,
And by dusk there'll seem to be enough
To throw open the sash by themselves.
Despite Old Gabe's new window, somehow
A few fly inside. I've taken to plucking
Them up with the vacuum. Seems a bit more
Humane than crushing them. At least they smell
Like decent creatures, not like those awful
Shield-shaped undesirable immigrants
That last year showed up uninvited, unwelcome,
Sitting like smallpox scars on the side of the house.
I much prefer ladybugs. They don't stink, I think.

Wood Hens

A wood-pecking pair nests on Huff Island—
Probably the same birds I hear behind the house.
They fly across the river like a flattened sine wave,
Flap, dip, flap, dip. Mama called them wood hens,
As did Posey. When I got my first bird book,
I didn't know if they were pile-e-ated
Or pill-e-ated. Good old *Webster's* Second said
Long *i* was preferred. (So, pile-e-ated,
Not to be confused with Old Gabe's mylomo bird,
Which, when it hollers, can be heard a mile or more.)
At the apex of my ideal totem pole would be
The alpha woodpecker—red crest, white neck,
Attitude. (How much more did the ivorybill have,
The creature people called Lord God Bird?)
Hope we have sense enough to leave woods enough
For the pileateds to flourish. I'd hate to think
They'd go extinct, leave the planet, die off,
Like dodoes or Carolina parakeets or passenger pigeons.
That is all too common these fraught days.

Asheville

Hotels and traffic snarls. Subarus.
Cotton candy–colored hair. Tattoos.
Skateboarders. Nose (and other things) rings.
Breweries. Food festivals. Tourists. Beer.
Friday night drum circles. Protests.
Topless rallies. Pride parades and Mardi Gras.
(Did I ever mention breweries?)
All this, except a beer or two, I avoid.
Still, there's Malaprop's, which I go by
Every month or two. Each October
I visit Thomas Wolfe and his colorful kin
At Riverside, where it's relatively quiet.
Otherwise I stick close to the Tennessee line,
Where life in the slow lane suits me fine.

Hot Springs

The village's first English name was Warm Springs,
For the ancient mineral baths near the confluence
Of Spring Creek and the French Broad River.
Its Warm Springs Hotel, with thirteen white columns,
One for each state, attracted the rich and famous.
About a century before I moved here, while adding
To the hotel, another fissure was found, the water
From which was eight or ten degrees warmer.
So they renamed the town. (Makes one wonder
About Cleveland County's Boiling Springs.)
The Warm Springs Hotel became the Mountain Park.
After it burned, was rebuilt, and burned again,
It joined a long list of used-to-bes in the town.
(Dorland-Bell School, Plemmons Hotel, etc.)
The boosters who heated up the name
Would not have imagined the Appalachian Trail,
Or that any right-minded person would hike
Georgia to Maine (or the other way around).
But hikers stop in Hot Springs for a shower and hot meal
And general delivery mail. A village of some five hundred souls,
Its growth is constrained by geography.
In summer it's lively with festivals and music.
So far it isn't as weird as Asheville, but I suspect
It will soon have a brewery. I go in every now and then,
Willingly to the public library, Gentry Hardware,
And the Smoky Mountain Diner—the Dollar General
When I have to. But I'm happy to live five miles
Downstream. Don't care for crowds, even small ones.

Note: Hot Springs would become nearly perfect with a liquor store.
It's a long way to Weaverville.

July Fourth

From my porch I hear the fireworks
Five miles up the road in Hot Springs.
But here the lovely fireflies dance,
Quietly, bouncy, looking for love
Beside the trees near the river.
I prefer the lightning bugs, as Posey
Named them. They flash with no
Noise, annoyance, gunpowder odor.
And after the loudness ends,
They keep their courtship vigil.

Ditch Lilies

Yellow and orange
Texts to be read silently
Annunciations all.

Fire Pinks

Behold their edges
Sheared as if for festive dress
Then they bleed crimson.

Trilliums (Trillia?)

A patch of three-leaved
Loveliness suddenly graces
The northside roadbank.

Wild Iris

Blue and yellow flags
On the logging road planted
By no one but God.

July Evening

After a hot day, a threat of rain brought
A fleeting eastern rainbow, partial arc
Over the river floating so ineffably—
Then—as if God chose to go herself one better—
Sunset exploded on the western sky,
Violent pinks and subtle golds shouted,
Where were you when I made these clouds?
Before I even thought to get my camera
It vanished into Tennessee, sun colors chased
By a by-now-only-remembered rainbow.
Well.
As they say around here, *She done good.*

Bad Words

Time was, I read certain magazines
And never encountered certain words.
They were, literally, unprintable.
Don't get me wrong—I'm no prude,
And when I stub my toe or drop my toast
On the wrong side I can turn the air blue.
But there are certain words I'd just as soon not find
When I read for edification.
But these days you can't avoid them.
Not certain that's untrammeled progress.
It might be time for a little editorial regress,
When we can remember the girl from Nantucket
Kept all her bad words in her (symbolic) bucket.

Note: When they replace "*$%#*&+!!" (Did you know those are called "grawlixes"?) with actual words, I'll have to quit reading the comics.

Tax Dollars

I'm used to finding fishermen at what I call
The Catfish Hole, but today four pickup trucks
Blocked the road there, to put in a strange boat.
Two trucks owned by the feds, two by the state.
Five or six young men seemed pleased
To be paid to spend a day on the river
In a soft boat rigged with two metal poles
Connected to a battery. From each pole's end
A metal water strider dangled like some strange
Christmas ornament. The men meant to collect
As many sucker fish as they could shock,
Then transplant them far upstream to waters
The poor fish used to inhabit. I didn't say
That maybe the fish had left upstream
For good reasons. I was polite and positive,
But wondered what Posey would say. Likely
A gripe about government messing with nature.
(After all, a river will, if left alone, balance itself.)
Still, I'd rather my tax dollars pay these do-good boys
Than buy more bombs, bullets, and bazookas.
How many fish did they finally find?
I'm sure their catch was quite stunning.

Drought

It's only rained two inches since summer.
Now, in November, the river is as low
As I have seen, over two feet down.
The only benefit is that more exposed rocks
Mean more river racket, so I'm rocked to sleep.
But it's scary. Maybe good for herons who breakfast here,
But I worry about fires, farmers, and crowded fish.
This drought is like having a rock in your shoe—
When you can't stop running to get rid of it.
Lord, we need rain. Oh, I know it will come,
But sooner rather than later, please.

Four-Inch Rain

It's so dry that from my porch I see
Lots and lots of river rocks like sore thumbs
Pointing accusingly skyward, demanding rain.
Upstream, grass grows on an island as big
As a pickup bed, usually hidden by the flow,
A fine place for bass to hold, where food
Will fill their smallmouths. Don't know
Where the fish are now. Gone fishing?
Today we had what I'd call a dusting of rain.
Old Gabe knew a man who, after such events,
Would say they'd had a four-inch rain.
When you looked at him like he was nuts,
He'd say, *One drop ever four inches*, and slap his knee.
It isn't funny, though. So dry a tossed cigarette
Might start a thousand-acre brush fire.
Jesus said to ask, so every day I do,
And hope for enough rain to re-cover these rocks,
To replenish the river, to restore its natural rhythm.
Waiting, with Elijah and the widow,
For the heavenly blessing of rain.

Black Vultures

A partnership of buzzards
In graceful airborne dance,
Reveling in an unseen stench—

Sunshine warming bodies black
As frock coats, wingtips white
As biscuit dough—
Perhaps a formal smell
Demands they dress for dinner.

January Twenty-Second

This is the day of my granny's borning,
Ruined forty years ago this morning
Because her son, my father, died—a day so grim,
In which she sobbed and wailed and cried—but not for him.
She moaned that he her day did spoil
Which only made my young blood boil.
I never spoke to her again
(He and I still talk every now and then)
Nor did I go to her funeral years later.
I suppose I'd grown to love to hate her.
Miss him? Still do, every day.
Miss her? Not one little bit, I'd say.
I pray heaven's an enormous place
So I'll not have to see her face.
Were we to meet beside the river,
I'd have no choice—but to forgive her.

Soup

One fine thing I do is turn random foods
Into soup. Not unlike herding random words
Into poetry. Poems and soups nourish
Body and soul alike. Soups are easy.
Potato soup is full of roots and onions
And half-and-half. Chicken noodle is
Swell if I have enough celery and carrots.
In summer, gazpacho honors ripe tomatoes,
Peppers, and onions with a bit of balsamic
And a soupçon of pepper sauce.
My cold-weather favorite is vegetable beef.
Simmer stew beef, marrow bone, and tomato juice
With any veggies from fridge, freezer, or cabinet.
Spice with bay leaf, and (my secret) lots of basil.
It's harder to throw words into a pot
And hope that what results will preach.
Words often won't obey the laws of
Thermodynamics, but when they do, the poem
Smells good, tastes great, and fills the soul
With something like word-rich gumbo.
Goulash. Cioppino. Bouillabaisse.
Stuff to stick to your spiritual ribs.

Winter Storm

Waiting for a winter storm, I smile,
I scan the sky for signs of snow or sleet,
What Posey deemed as "falling weather."
Wispy pre-snow clouds, shifting breeze.
I walk by the river and spy no kingfisher,
Heron, goose, nor duck. Perhaps birds know.
I listen to the weather band, then drive
To Marshall with more than half the county,
Where I buy no "light bread" (that shelf's
Bare as a birch twig) but stock up
On meat and wine and olives and cheese.
I have oak and maple and sweet gum,
And a stove in which to burn them. I have
Dried beans and cornmeal and ground chuck.
The storm may hit. Or fizzle out. Whatever
Happens, I'm ready. Watchful. Always.

Cold Feet

Lately it's been cold here. No matter
How tight Old Gabe fixed up my house,
Or how warm my woodstove gets, or how well
The heat pump works, I still come down with
Cold feet. My surefire remedy? A rice bag.
A small flannel sack full of rice, sewn shut.
After three or four microwave minutes
It is toasty, and either rests atop my feet or goes
Undercover at the foot of my bed, so all is well.

The other day, outside temperature fifteen above,
Across the river I spied a thin blue column.
Binoculars focused a great blue heron
In frigid water at Huff Island's edge,
Looking for all the world as if its shoulders
Were hunched in disgust at the weather,
Wondering if frog, fish, or snake would grace its sight.
Or had they taken the day off, so it should, too?
I smiled, and wondered if it would fancy
A rice bag to warm its icy yellow feet.

Cherry Tree

Midwinter, too warm, a thunderstorm,
Wind, rain, and even a bit of hail.
Something not lightning popped outside.
I started to the back door just as a tree
From up the mountain crashed to ground,
Its topnotch not ten feet from the house.
Next day I saw it was a wild cherry
And called Old Gabe, who came that week,
Eyeballed the tree, and chuckled.
Limby dang thing, ain't it?
He lopped some limbs and said he'd be back
Soon to finish. The root ball was torn out of the ground,
So I marveled to see the remaining limbs budding.
Reminded me of a ballad we studied in college,
About Joseph, Mary, and a cherry tree, which,
When Gabe returned, I mentioned. He nodded.
Mama used to sing that to me. How'd it go?
He spat on the ground, cleared his throat, and sang:
Then bowed down the highest tree,
Unto his mother's hand;
Then she cried, See, Joseph,
I have cherries at command.
He shook his head and picked up his saw.
Miss Susan, you'll get no cherries
From this here tree. Still, I've knowed them
To put out leaves in spite of lopped limbs.
I smiled. *Go ahead and cut it up. I doubt*
This is a miracle tree. Take all you want
For pay. Of course, he didn't take a bit,

And took away the slash. I was simply glad the tree
Missed the house—and lost its bid to be
Fuel for a Madison County balladeer.
My woodstove is miracle enough for me.

Silver Bells

The music of spring
Decorates the thin branches
Like white ornaments.

Joe-Pye Weed

Tall ditch-bound bloomer
Bowing in pink prayer-like nod
Full of bees and hope.

Cardinal Flower

Not vestments but bright
Red birds hinge us to scarlet
Blossoms of God's love.

Ferns

At least a dozen
Species grace River Road's bank
With green angel wings.

Tomcat

Every now and then I'm asked why I don't have a dog.
Subtext? Aren't you lonesome way out here?
I say, *I get along fine without a dog.* The real answer
Is knotty. I grew up with dogs. I've never been dogbit,
As Posey would put it. But he's the reason I own no dog.
When he died, Tomcat, his hound and spaniel
And Lord knew what else, grieved
Like an inconsolable human.
Posey's son, Tim, took Tomcat home, but
A day or two later he was back, sniffing
For his friend. The third time he showed up
I asked Tim if he didn't want me to take the dog.
So I became Tomcat's second best friend,
And when I bought Eagle Bluff he moved
More or less happily with me. Oh, he was no
Blithe spirit. A dozen years old when Posey passed,
He was likelier to bark at squirrels than chase them.
But he protected me, and we loved each other.
When he was sixteen and getting down in his hips
I fretted about when to call the vet, but one day
The doggone dog was—gone. I called and called
And searched and searched but never found him.
I cried, as e.e. said, like the Missouri, and after that
My dog days ended. I'll not go through that again.
I doubt that canines go to heaven,
But it's fine to think of Posey and Birdie
Walking together, Tomcat protecting their flank.
(What threats lurk there is a dogmatic question,
But I know Tomcat would take no chances.)
So, no, I don't have a dog, and, no, I'm not lonesome.
The ghosts who crowd my head are ample company.

Fugitives

They came skulking up the road like stragglers
From a Grimm tale. I was on the porch,
Just finished morning müseli, feeling full.
He was a Lester Ballard–looking young man, severely
Skinny, hatchet face and beard and hair
That looked cut with a hedge trimmer. Might have been thirty.
She was chunky, straight obsidian black hair.
Might have been twenty. He wore pajama bottoms
With some kind of cartoonish pattern. She carried
A light-colored cloth bag that could have held
Clothing or a sawed-off shotgun wrapped in burlap.
They stopped—he looked up at me. *How far to town?*
He asked. *Five miles*, I said. *Can you take us there?*
We run out of gas back at that fish pond. Flat,
Country accent, but not Carolina—maybe Arkansas.
She was silent, staring east like she expected the apocalypse.
Sure, I said. *I'll be just a minute.* I went inside, seeing
They had no gas can, put pistol in handbag, and locked up.
They waited at my car like this was a normal Thursday morning.

On the way to town I tried small talk
But she sat silent in the back seat. He didn't reveal
Anything, except he sure didn't know where he was.
Neither smelled like they were headed to a ballroom dance.
I kept an eye on her, but she made no move toward the bag
Stashed in her lap. Mine was close to my left hand.
I left them at the caboose that doubled as a welcome center.
As he got out he told her they needed to find a church to help them.
She thanked me. He didn't. When I headed back, they were walking
Toward the outfitter's store, but they didn't seem to belong
With hikers on the Appalachian Trail.

Next morning I decided to breakfast at the diner. Halfway down
River Road a deputy blocked the road. He asked
If I'd seen a teenaged girl and showed me a picture
Of yesterday's passengers. She had been reported missing
In Missouri. She was thirteen. I told him what I remembered,
And we agreed to continue the interview at the diner.
When I said I'd seen them at the outfitter's,
He excused himself and headed out the door. As I was finishing
Eggs and grits and hash browns, he came back, said
They remembered the boy because of his Batman britches.
They had caught a ride in a white pickup to Asheville,
And the deputy seemed ready to hand this off to Buncombe police
And go back to doing whatever Madison County deputies normally do.

The next Tuesday's Asheville newspaper reported
They had been caught in a Transylvania County campground.
He was in jail—she had been returned to her guardian.
Made me wonder. What if they had pulled a weapon
And shot or stabbed me before I could reach mine,
Left me bleeding or worse in a ditch? What if I had refused
Their request? What if I'd been inside when they walked by?
And a troubling question—did I do the right thing? I know
It's wrong to kidnap anyone, much less a young girl.
But what if she regarded him as some strange savior,
Removing her from an unbearable situation?
She never resembled a victim, unless one of
Poverty, or abuse. I'll never know. I'm simply happy
They didn't harm me. I'll add them to my little list.
They sure are, as the spiritual says, standing in the need of prayer.

That Didn't End Right

Our family's first TV arrived the year
I left for college. Mostly cabinet, it sported
A small round screen we crowded close to see.
When I was home on break, I'd watch,
With my parents, whatever was on:
Bozo the Clown, Ozzie and Harriet,
Candid Camera, Dragnet, Jack Benny.
My favorite show was *I Love Lucy.*
I remember well my mother, after watching a western,
Cisco Kid maybe, moving toward the kitchen,
Saying, *That didn't end right.* By which she meant
The bad guys were not punished (enough),
And the good guys were not rewarded (enough).
Pretty much summed her view of how the world
Should be, albeit pretty far from where it was then.
Fifty-odd years later, things seem much worse.
Soon we all might be led to exclaim—
That didn't end right!—when our world's going up in flames.

Cherry Casket

A week after first frost, I decided to make
A batch of vegetable soup. I'd just finished
When Old Gabe dropped by to leave
A jar of beautiful persimmon jelly
He'd put up last week. I gave him a quart
Of soup, then we sat on the porch in the sun.
I have a project for you, I said.
You fixing to add on? he asked,
Blue eyes twinkling. *No, I'm past that.*
I want you to make me a casket.
He cocked one eyebrow at me. *For what?*
I smiled. *For me, silly. I want to be buried*
Back of the house up the hill so I can
Hear the river. He nodded slowly, looked
Toward living water. *You all in a sweat for this?*
I laughed. *No, but I just turned seventy,*
And you know what the Book says about that.
He smiled. *I do, indeed. You're sure?*
Definitely, I said. He leaned forward
And put his hands on his knees. *Well, Miss Susan,*
You got to lie a hundred foot from your well.
I'll check how far you got to be from the river.
I got some mighty fine cherry planks
I didn't know I was saving for you.
They'd make a right smart-looking coffin.
You want a squared-off box, or tapered
Like them old-timey ones? Not having thought about that,
I tilted my head toward him. *Tapered, I suppose.*
He nodded. *You want a shroud? Or maybe a dress?*

I chuckled. *Gabe, you ever see me in a dress?*
No, but you never know. I had an aunt one time
Who just had to be buried in her wedding dress.
They had to cut it all up to fit it in the coffin.
He scratched his chin. *Where you figure to store it?*
In the spare bedroom. I'm not going to sleep
In it, like the old poet John Donne did.
That the Dunn with a funeral home up in Asheville?
No, Gabe, he was an English poet. A preacher, too.
Well, that's too many for me, he sighed. *Miss Susan,*
I got to ask you to stand up so I can measure you out.
So I did, and he did, and we sat back down in some
Small embarrassment. *How much will this cost?*
He shook his head. *I wouldn't dare charge you a nickel.*
It's an honor you even asked me to help you out.

Two weeks later he showed up with a beautiful box,
Shiny, with an oil finish. He was rightly proud of it.
Miss Susan, them joints is tighter'n Dick's hatband.
You needn't fret about water coming in for a long time.

I called the funeral home in Marshall,
Prepaid their services. Now all I have to do
Is die at home so I won't trouble anyone.
I'm not afraid to die but am a bit scared
Of the process, if prologue is pain and suffering.
If it comes to that, I have pills and alcohol plenty.
It will be another adventure to wake to what's next.
They will have an everlasting abundance
Of red wine, dark chocolate, and vine-ripe tomatoes.
If they don't, I'll know where my soul has gone.

Seventies

In my seventies, my "twilight years."
Won't live forever, at least I hope not.
But I have no regrets to speak of.
My house is paid for, I'm comfortably set,
My funeral is arranged. In my time
I have delighted in God's creation,
And made some verses which folks have read
With profit and delight, no trivial thing.
Poesis is creation—and poetry
Tries its best to dovetail with God's making beauty.
To add to creation instead of subtract
Is all the monument I need to leave.
As the Bard said, *Ripeness is all.*
As Mehitabel the Cat said,
i ain't got any regrets
for i gave my life to my art,
So I'm ready for whatever is next.

Dreams

I don't dream much, at least that I remember.
When a kid I dreamed of flying, or falling,
But it's been decades since that happened.
Every blue moon or so I see my parents,
Always at the house where I grew up.
Best I can tell, they're happy, or at least
Not suffering. After Posey passed
I dreamed about him fairly often,
But not so much now. He's always calm,
Smiling, saying, *Be Careful, Now.*
Which, as I woke the other day I realized
Was his old man's way of saying,
I love you. That has stayed with me
A long time. I don't much believe in heaven,
And certainly don't believe in hell,
But I do think there's something else,
Where all will be well. Maybe dreams can
Access that future. Anyway, I seem
To hold out hope I'll see my old friend again,
Somehow. So I'm careful. I really am,
Because I'd like that to happen.
Posey, you be careful, now, too.

ACKNOWLEDGMENTS

After *Woodsmoke*, I left a chair on my mental porch for Posey. He didn't come back to talk. I tried to replicate his voice, but the poems were, as he would have said, deader'n doornails.

So I welcomed Susan to that chair. *River Road* is the fruit of our musings. Hope I haven't heard the last from her.

Thanks to the team at Blair, folks who know what they are doing. Special thanks to Robin Miura, the best editor I have had the pleasure of working with.

A heartfelt thanks to the late Fred Chappell, who, despite declining health, read these poems, made his usual sharp suggestions, and gave this volume maybe the last cover blurb he ever wrote. Mentor in many ways, rest in peace, Ole Fred.

As usual, thanks to the Holden Beach Writer's Conference, who listened to these poems around various and sundry tables.

And, always, thanks to Mary, without whose love and support none of this would happen.